EXQUISITE TRAVEL GUIDE SERIES

ST. KITTS AND NEVIS

TRAVEL GUIDE 2024

INSIDE:
- PICTURES
- INSIDER TIPS
AND MANY MORE

ALL YOU NEED TO KNOW ABOUT THE KITTITIANS AND NEVISIANS CULTURE, TOP MUST-SEE DESTINATION, INSIDER TIPS FOR SOLO TRAVELLERS, FAMILIES, SENIORS AND FIRST-TIME VISITORS

ROLAND RICHARD

ST. Kitts and Nevis Travel Guide 2024

All You Need To Know About the Kittitians and Nevisians Culture, Top Must-See Destination, Insider Tips for Solo Travellers, Families, Seniors and First-Time Visitors

ROLAND RICHARD

Copyright 2023. Roland Richard.

All rights Reserved!

No part of this book may be reproduced, stored in a retrieval system, or transmitted in any form or by any means, electronic, mechanical, photocopying, recording, or otherwise, without the prior written permission of the copyright owner.

Table of Contents

Table of Contents	3
St Kitts and Nevis Map	6
My Personal Experience	7
Introduction	11
Overview of St Kitts and Nevis	12
Purpose of the Travel Guide	13
Quick Facts about the Kittitians and Nevisians' Culture	13
CHAPTER 1	
Essential Travel Information	16
Requirements for Visas	17
Money and Banking	17
Language and Communication	18
CHAPTER 2	
Planning Your Trip	20
When Is the Best to Go?	20
Climate and Weather	20
Things You Need To Pack	21
Health and Safety Tips	22
CHAPTER 3	
Cultural Insights	24
Understanding Kittitians and Nevisian Culture	24
Local Customs and Etiquette	25
Festivals and Events	27
CHAPTER 4	
Top Must-See Destinations	31
Basseterre: The Capital City	31

> Brimstone Hill Fortress National Park — 32
> Hike to Nevis Peak — 34
> Coastal Attractions & Beaches — 35

CHAPTER 5
Activities and Experiences — 38
> Water-Based Adventure and Sports — 38
> Museums and Historical Tours — 39
> Gastronomic Delights: Nevisian and Kittitian Cuisine — 40

CHAPTER 6
Expert Tips for Solo Travelers — 43
> Safety Advice for Solo Travellers — 43
> Getting to Know Locals and Establishing Connections — 46

CHAPTER 7
Perfect Adventures for the Family — 49
> Kid-Friendly Attractions — 49
> Family-Friendly Resorts — 50
> Activities for All Ages — 52

CHAPTER 8
Travelling as Seniors — 56
> Senior-Friendly Accommodations and Transportation — 56
> Transportation Suitable for Seniors: — 56
> Health Considerations for Seniors — 57
> Relaxing Activities and Leisurely Tours — 58

CHAPTER 9
Guide for First-Time Visitors — 61
> Arrival and Airport Tips — 61
> Exchange of Currency — 62
> Navigating Public Transportation — 62

Common Tourist Mistakes to Avoid	64

CHAPTER 10

Sample Itineraries	67
3-Day Adventure Itinerary	67
5-Day Cultural Immersion Itinerary	70
Relaxing Beach Retreat: A 7-Day Itinerary	74

CHAPTER 11

Useful Resources	77
Emergency Contacts	77
Suggested Reading and Additional Details	80

CONCLUSION

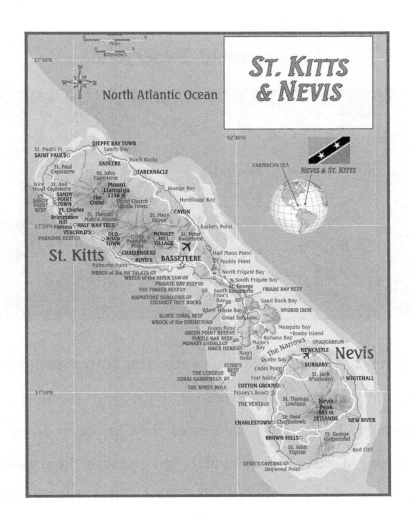

St Kitts and Nevis Map

My Personal Experience

It felt like I had walked into a very real dream when I first set foot on the beaches of St. Kitts and Nevis. I was welcomed by the lively colours of the Caribbean, from the bustling markets full of handcrafted goods of the region to the irresistible perfume of spicy food and the warm smiles of the people of Basseterre, the dynamic capital of St. Kitts.

The invitation to fully immerse myself in the genuine rhythm of the islands came right away.

Climbing Brimstone Hill Fortress was like a trip back in time. From this vantage position, one could not help but be astounded by the expansive vistas of the Caribbean Sea, which met a verdant patchwork of landscapes. Strolling throughout Basseterre's historic alleys uncovered little-known treasures, such as lively waterfront areas teeming with local activity and centuries-old churches echoing with stories from the past.

I quickly took a ferry to Nevis, which took me to a slower, more tranquil environment. Every worn brick in Charlestown's narrow alleyways seemed to whisper stories of the island's rich past, making it feel like a journey through history. Nevis Peak's imposing presence gave the island's allure a magnificent touch.

The St. Kitts Music Festival exceeded all expectations as a celebration. Everyone was drawn to the dance floor by the lively music, which was a blend of soca and reggae beats, which shone beneath the shimmering Caribbean stars. It was more than simply a musical spectacle; it was a genuine look into the vibrant, hospitable, and energetic existence of the Kittitians.

Taking a culinary tour of the area was a sensory extravaganza. Every mouthful was a tasty excursion through the history and cultural influences of the islands, from savouring freshly caught seafood delicacies to indulging in substantial "Goat Water" stew at a modest beach shack.

St. Kitts and Nevis' beaches were practically picture-perfect. Scuba diving and snorkelling revealed a vivid kaleidoscope of marine life beneath the surface, while the powder-white sands gave way to crystal-clear turquoise waters.

There was a pinch of regret as it came time to say goodbye to St. Kitts and Nevis. My inner self has been permanently transformed by the people's friendliness, the music's contagious beats, and the breathtaking beauty of the surroundings. It was an immersive experience that felt real and magical, not just a holiday.

St. Kitts and Nevis have become essential parts of my journey, rather than just points on a map. It was a vow to come back, a determination to find more of the islands' undiscovered gems and make even more priceless memories in this paradise in the Caribbean. This travel guide is a carefully curated collection of my experiences and research.

Be prepared to be mesmerised!

Introduction

Embark on discovering St. Kitts and Nevis, an irresistible paradise in the centre of the Caribbean where crystal-clear waters, natural surroundings, and a vibrant cultural legacy combine in harmony to provide an experience that travellers will never forget. It was a profound journey for me to explore these islands, and I'm excited to share the knowledge and insights I discovered along the way.

Overview of St Kitts and Nevis

St. Kitts: The Pulsating Heart

St. Kitts, the larger of the two islands, with its vibrant city of Basseterre, greets you with open arms. This thriving centre combines colourful marketplaces, historic sites, and the friendly bustle of everyday life. Explore the local markets, climb the old Brimstone Hill Fortress for sweeping vistas, and let the calypso beats of the music direct your route.

Nevis: The Peaceful Haven

Nevis, which is only a short ferry trip away, has a more relaxed vibe and is home to the famous Nevis Peak. Take in the leisurely pace of life, see quaint plantations, and relax on immaculate beaches. Nevis extends an invitation for relaxation amidst stunning scenery and intriguing history.

Purpose of the Travel Guide

This travel guide is a travel companion designed to improve your experience, not just a list of suggestions. This book is designed to satisfy your needs, whether you're a family looking for happy moments, a solitary traveller seeking adventure, or an elderly traveller wanting peace. You can anticipate well-chosen insights, insider knowledge, and useful guidance to make your trip to St. Kitts & Nevis simple and enriching.

Quick Facts about the Kittitians and Nevisians' Culture

Experience Warmth and Hospitality

Its people's friendly smiles and inviting nature are the beating heart of St. Kitts and Nevis. Get ready to experience a culture that embodies hospitality with pride. Participate in colourful festivals alongside the islanders, where traditional dances and music reflect the energy of island life.

Culinary Delights

Discover the tastes of Kittitian and Nevisian cooking, which combines French, British, and African flavours. Savour regional delicacies like "Johnny Cakes" and "Goat Water" stew. Eating here is a cultural immersion as well as a gastronomic one.

Celebrations and Festivals

Schedule your trip during colourful celebrations like the Nevis Mango & Food Festival or the St. Kitts Music Festival. These gatherings offer a chance to celebrate life with the locals while showcasing the cultural diversity of the islands.

You can expect a genuine experience with St. Kitts and Nevis's soul as we embark on this journey. The secret spots, intriguing cultural details, and breathtaking natural features that make these islands such a unique travel destination may all be found with the help of this book. Prepare to learn the mysteries of this paradisal Caribbean island.

Overlooking Brimstone Hill fortress

Chapter 1
Essential Travel Information

To guarantee a smooth and pleasurable trip, you must obtain essential travel information before leaving for St. Kitts and Nevis. To begin with, take note of the local time zone and modify your timetable accordingly.

In case of an emergency, keep a record of the important contacts, such as the embassy or consulate of your nation.

Furthermore, keep both hard copy and digital copies of all the key documents you own, such as your passport, travel insurance, and reservation confirmations.

Requirements for Visas

An important part of organising your vacation is understanding the visa requirements. While many nationalities can enter St. Kitts and Nevis without a visa for brief visits, it's important to confirm the exact rules based on your citizenship. Get the right visa if you plan to stay for a long time. For the most recent and accurate information, stay informed by visiting the official government website or getting in touch with the closest embassy.

Money and Banking

Having a thorough understanding of local currencies and banking options guarantees that you have the money you need for trouble-free travel. The national currency is the

Eastern Caribbean Dollar (XCD), therefore it's helpful to know the current exchange rates.

Major credit cards are accepted everywhere, but to prevent any disruptions in card usage, it's a good idea to let your bank know when you'll be travelling. Urban locations are home to ATMs, which offer easy access to cash for daily requirements.

Language and Communication

Since English is the official language of St. Kitts and Nevis, most visitors will find it easy to communicate there. The residents' unique Caribbean accents lend a pleasant element to discussions.

Learn a few simple phrases in the regional tongue to better interact with the people. Kind words of appreciation and a simple 'Good morning' will go a long way towards building strong bonds with the hospitable Kittitians and Nevisians.

Explore these key points to make your trip even more enjoyable. Establishing your familiarity with the local time, currency, linguistic quirks, and visa procedures will help you have a well-planned and engaging journey through the enthralling scenery and welcoming locals of St. Kitts and Nevis.

Chapter 2

Planning Your Trip

When Is the Best to Go?

To get the most out of your visit to St. Kitts and Nevis, timing is everything. December through April, when tourism is at its peak, delivers nice weather with low humidity and little rain. The shoulder seasons of May to June and September to November can be attractive if you're looking for a more peaceful vibe and don't mind experiencing the occasional rainfall. Remember that June through November is hurricane season, so it's a good idea to be informed about weather predictions during this time.

Climate and Weather

As a result of its tropical environment, St. Kitts and Nevis have pleasant weather all year round. Average daytime temperatures are between 80°F and 88°F (27°C and 31°C).

December through April is the dry season on the islands, and May through November is the wet season. Rain showers can occur occasionally, especially during the wet season, so be ready for them. Having rain gear and light, breathable clothing with you can ensure that you stay comfortable in any weather.

Things You Need To Pack

Take into account the tropical weather and the things you want to do when preparing for your trip. Important things consist of:

1. *Light Clothes:* To stay cool in the summer, bring breathable materials like cotton and linen.
2. *Swimwear:* Wear proper swimwear to enjoy the stunning beaches and water sports.

3. *Sun Protection:* To protect oneself from the Caribbean sun, pack a wide-brimmed hat, sunglasses, and sunscreen.
4. *Insect Repellent:* Although mosquitoes are usually not a big deal, carrying repellent can be helpful, particularly if you intend to walk or explore nature reserves.
5. *Comfort Shoes:* It's important to wear comfy shoes whether you're hiking the trails or taking strolls through historic places.
6. *Travel Adapters:* Considering St. Kitts & Nevis uses Type A and B electrical plugs, make sure you have the correct adapters for your equipment.

Health and Safety Tips

Make your health and safety a priority by paying attention to these tips:

1. *Immunisations:* Before departing, find out which immunisations are advised by your healthcare professional.
2. *Stay Hydrated:* Bring a reusable water bottle because the warm weather requires it.
3. *Local Cuisine Caution:* While it's imperative to try the meal, exercise caution when consuming street food, and make sure the fish and water come from reputable sources.
4. *Safety Advice:* Keep an eye out for potential threats, especially in less frequented places, and lock up your possessions to prevent small-time theft.

You can create the ideal conditions for a joyful and worry-free exploration of the breathtaking landscapes and dynamic culture of St. Kitts and Nevis by carefully organising your trip, considering the weather, packing sensibly, and placing a high priority on health and safety.

Chapter 3
Cultural Insights

Understanding Kittitians and Nevisian Culture

Warm Hospitality

The gracious hospitality shown to guests is the cornerstone of Kittitian and Nevisian culture. Locals enjoy making visitors feel at home and frequently strike up a nice discussion. This kind of hospitality is a year-round feature that adds charm to each visit. If you are asked into a local home or given a sample of traditional food, don't be shocked by it.

Cultural Pride

St. Kitts and Nevis residents are extremely proud of their culture. Their genuine excitement for sharing their heritage with guests is evident in everything from their vivid music and dance to their historical landmarks. Take advantage of the chance to learn about the rich past, and try to time your visit to coincide with festivals and events to see how much they value their culture.

Local Customs and Etiquette

Greetings and Respect

Greet someone with a "Good morning" or "Good afternoon," then extend a handshake to start a conversation.

Unless otherwise requested, using titles like Mr., Mrs., or Miss is considered courteous.

Elderly people are highly respected, and it's traditional to treat them with respect. This respect is a fundamental component of local etiquette, as it is strongly incorporated into everyday interactions.

Dress Modestly

Even though the islands have a relaxed vibe, it is respectful to wear modest clothing, particularly while visiting places of worship of cultural significance.

This shows consideration for regional traditions. Bringing a small gift when you are invited into someone's home is a kind gesture and a way to say thank you for the hospitality.

Island Time

Life at St Kitts and Nevis moves at a leisurely "island time" pace. It is recommended that visitors have a calm and relaxed demeanour, bearing in mind that things could proceed more slowly than in busier settings. People who take the time to appreciate moments and relationships in daily interactions are particularly good at exhibiting this cultural trait.

Festivals and Events

St. Kitts Music Festival

The St. Kitts Music Festival honours the dynamic Caribbean music industry and is held in June every year. Performers from both local and global come together to provide a wide variety of musical styles. It's best to confirm the exact dates for the year you intend to come as the festival's dates sometimes change slightly.

Mango and Food Festival in Nevis

The Nevis Mango & Food Festival, which takes place in July, is a gastronomic extravaganza that showcases the distinctive tastes of Caribbean food, with a focus on the popular mango. It's a chance to sample a range of foods, learn about the regional culinary scene, and appreciate the depth of Nevisian cuisine. Check the schedule for the current year as the dates may differ.

Culturama (Nevis)

Culturama is a lively cultural event that takes place in late July or early August and includes parades, street dances, traditional performances, and many competitions. It offers a thorough exploration of Nevisian heritage, giving both residents and tourists a fully comprehensive cultural experience. When making travel plans, make sure you have the most recent schedule as the dates may change.

In addition to being entertaining, going to these festivals and events is a great way to meet people in the area, see different cultural expressions, and take part in the exuberant celebrations that characterise life in St. Kitts and Nevis.

Accepting these traditions and participating in local activities while keeping track of the dates will improve your trip and leave you with enduring memories of the islands' diverse cultures.

Chapter 4

Top Must-See Destinations

Basseterre: The Capital City

- *Address: Independence Square, Basseterre, St. Kitts*
- *GPS Coordinates: 17.2962° N, 62.7307° W*

Explore Historic Charm

Explore the fascinating history of Basseterre, the vibrant capital of St. Kitts. Not only is Independence Square a significant historical site, but it's also a lively community centre with a contagious vibe.

Explore The National Museum, a veritable gold mine of relics detailing the intriguing past of the island, by strolling down Bay Road. At the Basseterre Public Market, indulge your senses with a sensory feast that combines the brilliant colours of local vegetables with the aromas of spices.

Cruise Port and Circus:

At the main cruise port, ***Port Zante***, feel the pulse of the city. Excitement permeates the air as guests peruse stores rich with local artwork. The Circus lends a humorous element to the city's appeal with its distinctive building influenced by Victorian design.

Brimstone Hill Fortress National Park

- *Address: Brimstone Hill, St. Kitts*

- *GPS Coordinates: 17.3404° N, 62.8015° W*

Perched magnificently above a volcanic slope, Brimstone Hill Fortress National Park transports visitors to a past events period.

In addition to providing a historical tour and breathtaking panoramic views, the stronghold is a reminder of the island's colonial heritage. Examining this impressive building's well-preserved architecture will help you to appreciate its strategic importance.

Scenic Railway Tour

Take the Scenic Railway Tour for a leisurely journey. This charming voyage runs through beautiful surroundings, offering a distinctive viewpoint of Brimstone Hill and the island's unspoiled splendour. Take in the simplicity and genuineness of the way of life in the area as you travel the tracks.

Hike to Nevis Peak

Challenge and Benefit

Climb the dormant volcano Nevis Peak, which welcomes travellers, to start an exciting experience. Starting at the base, the walk leads you through deep, vibrant rainforests. Excitement mounts as you climb, and when you reach the top, an amazing view of nearby islands greets you—a testament to your hard work.

Ancient Plantations

The ***Hermitage Plantation Inn*** is a charming place to stay at the base of Nevis Peak. This old inn offers a peaceful hideaway surrounded by tropical gardens, as well as a window into the island's past as a sugar plantation. Take in all the allure of a bygone era.

- *Address (Hermitage Plantation Inn): Hermitage Estate, Nevis*
- *GPS Coordinates (Hermitage Plantation Inn): 17.1568° N, 62.6063° W*

Coastal Attractions & Beaches

Turquoise water and white sand

Relax on the immaculate beaches of St. Kitts and Nevis and bask in the picture-perfect splendour of these islands. The pristine waves and fine white beaches of ***South Friars Bay*** *and Cockleshell Beach* provide the perfect environment for unwinding. Find out about *Frigate Bay* that has beach bars, lively energy, and a range of water sports for a livelier setting.

Shitten Bay Snorkelling

Explore Shitten Bay's beautiful underwater environment. This place is a snorkeler's dream come true because of the coral reefs and abundant aquatic life. Take in the vivid hues and amazing marine life below the surface.

- *Address (Cockleshell Beach): Cockleshell Bay, St. Kitts*
- *GPS Coordinates (Cockleshell Beach): 17.2350° N, 62.6853° W*

Make sure to record your experience at these places. These locations provide more than just sightseeing—an immersive adventure into the heart and soul of St. Kitts and Nevis awaits you whether you're enjoying the historical elegance of Basseterre, reaching the heights of Brimstone Hill, conquering Nevis Peak, or giving in to the temptation of sun-kissed beaches.

Take in the spirit of each place, let the journey unfold, and make memories that will last long after your travels are over.

Nevis Peak

Chapter 5

Activities and Experiences

Water-Based Adventure and Sports

Go for the thrills

At Shitten Bay, go snorkelling to explore St. Kitts and Nevis's underwater treasures. Visualise drifting over the glistening waters, encircled by vivid coral structures and tropical fish. Companies such as Dive St. Kitts provide equipment and knowledgeable insights into marine life for their supervised snorkelling tours.

Try making an attempt at scuba diving in White House Bay for a wilder experience. Businesses such as Pro Divers St. Kitts can take you on an underwater tour of shipwrecks, providing you with an insight into the maritime past of the Caribbean.

Sailing and Catamaran Adventures

Set off on a full-day sailing adventure with Leeward Islands Charters, exploring the shoreline and making snorkelling stops at Monkey Rock. As you take in the expansive vistas of the verdant coastline, experience the catamaran's gently swaying. This trip, which costs about $150 per person, combines leisure with exploring the seas, making it an unforgettable experience.

Museums and Historical Tours

Brimstone Hill Walking Tour

Take a guided walking tour of Brimstone Hill Fortress to travel back in time. By narrating battles and colonial history, local guides from Brimstone Hill Fortress National Park brilliantly bring the past back to life. The expansive views of the surrounding islands can be seen from the summit and are quite breathtaking. It costs about $15 to enter the fortress and gain entry to the museum and other historical locations in the park.

Discover The National Museum

Visit The National Museum in Basseterre to learn about Kittitian history in depth. To properly enjoy the exhibits, which include Arawak ceramics and antiquities from the colonial era, take a guided tour. With entrance fees of about $5, this is an affordable way to learn about the history and cultural legacy of the island.

Gastronomic Delights: Nevisian and Kittitian Cuisine

Roadside eateries and local markets

Savour the delectable food offerings in the Basseterre Public Market. Savour traditional street cuisine such as "saltfish and Johnny Cakes" while perusing the colourful vendors.

These tasty treats, which cost about $5, offer a flavour of real Kittitian food. Don't pass up the opportunity to sample the refreshing sweet coconut dumpling delight from a street vendor:

Plantation Dining

Enjoy a meal amid lush tropical gardens while taking in the historic beauty of Ottley's Plantation Inn. Enjoy delicacies like coconut prawns and spiny lobster, which run between $30 and $50 and highlight the blending of Caribbean and foreign flavours.

Similarly, The Hermitage serves dishes like mango-glazed Mahi Mahi and provides a unique dining experience in a Great House from the 17th century. A supper at The Hermitage costs between $40 and $60 per person.

Every event is designed to make enduring memories within an affordable price range, whether you're looking for adventure in the seas, learning about the island's fascinating history, or enjoying the varied flavours of Kittitian and Nevisian cuisine. During your Caribbean vacation, let the islands' natural beauty, historical significance, and exquisite food reveal themselves to you in a seamless manner.

National Museum in Basseterre

Chapter 6

Expert Tips for Solo Travelers

Safety Advice for Solo Travellers

Appreciate Local Knowledge

Learn from the locals as you set out on your solo journey in St. Kitts and Nevis. Even though the islands are generally safe, travelling worry-free can be achieved by taking a few measures.

Pay attention to your surroundings in busy places like Basseterre's Independence Square or Port Zante, especially after dark. To improve your overall safety, follow your intuition and use caution in less congested locations.

Safeguard Your Belongings

Safeguarding your possessions is crucial in crowded tourist areas like the bustling marketplace in Port Zante. To prevent pickpockets, go for a concealed money belt or a crossbody bag. Make sure your possessions are safe if you want to peruse the Basseterre Public Market for regional specialities so you may take in the vibrant ambience of the place worry-free.

Health Precautions

Even though the islands have state-of-the-art medical facilities, it could still be helpful to have a modest first aid pack. Bring basic medical supplies including band-aids, painkillers, and prescription prescriptions in case of minor medical emergencies when visiting natural reserves such as Black Rocks or Mount Liamuiga. Learn about the healthcare options available in your area to give yourself an additional measure of security.

Recommended Solo-Friendly Accommodations

Timothy Beach Resort

Location: Timothy Beach Resort, Frigate Bay

Timothy Beach Resort in Frigate Bay is a good option for a solitary traveller's getaway. Its seaside location allows you to relax and take in the breathtaking sights.

The convivial atmosphere of the resort facilitates easy conversation with other guests as you explore the neighbouring Frigate Bay Strip, which is lined with eateries and beach bars. For solo travellers, interacting with the kind staff and other visitors provides a welcoming atmosphere.

The Ocean Terrace Inn

Location: Ocean Terrace Inn, Basseterre

The quiet location of Ocean Terrace Inn, which overlooks Basseterre, is ideal for solitary visitors. After exploring all day, unwind on the patio or pool. The small-scale setting of the hotel promotes conversation among visitors. Make use of the shared spaces and interact with the friendly staff at Ocean Terrace Inn, which makes it a great place for travellers travelling solo.

Getting to Know Locals and Establishing Connections

Participate in Local Events

Explore community activities like the Nevis Mango & Food Festival and the St. Kitts Music Festival. These events offer a chance to mingle with locals while also showcasing the islands' colourful culture. Whether it's a street parade in Charlestown or a cultural event in Basseterre, you'll have opportunities to network as you get fully involved in the celebrations.

Visit Cafes And Bars To Socialise

Visit neighbourhood pubs like **Sprat Net Beach Bar** and **The Dock**, as well as cafes like **Rituals Coffee House**. These local favourites are well-liked because they provide a laid-back vibe. Start a discussion with other customers or friendly employees. These locations' casual atmosphere makes it easy to meet both locals alongside other travellers.

Take Part in Workshops and Tours

Participate in courses or guided excursions to enhance your solo travels. Think about taking a historical walking tour of Basseterre or taking a culinary class with a local chef. Participating in group activities offers you the chance to meet people who share your interests and improves your comprehension of the islands.

Whether it's a historical workshop at the Alexander Hamilton Museum or a nature expedition to explore the rainforest, these events provide opportunities to make new acquaintances.

Indulging in the hospitality of the locals is just as important as touring the islands when travelling solo in St. Kitts and Nevis.

These islands embrace solitary travellers with open arms, making for an enriching and unforgettable experience. To start, make sure you observe safety precautions, select accommodations that are suitable for single travellers, and get involved with the local way of life.

Chapter 7

Perfect Adventures for the Family

Kid-Friendly Attractions

St. Kitts Scenic Railway

Take the family on an exciting journey on the St. Kitts Scenic Railway. This charming narrow-gauge railway offers breathtaking views of the island's scenery and shoreline as it winds around the island. Children of all ages can have a fun and pleasant experience in the open-air carriages. This is the perfect approach for the whole family to enjoy St. Kitts' natural beauty together.

The cost of the St. Kitts Scenic Railway excursion is roughly $110 for adults and $55 for children. Generally speaking, children under three travel free. This price includes drinks, a beautiful train trip, and a fun way for kids to take in St. Kitts' natural beauty.

Basseterre Public Market

Visit the Basseterre Public Market with your family to introduce them to St. Kitts' lively cultural scene. Explore the vibrant booths showcasing local merchants' fresh vegetables, handicrafts, and spices. Take your kids on a sensory tour of the sights and smells of the market. The market offers a genuine experience of island life in a bustling, kid-friendly setting.

While entry is free, fresh produce and locally produced food can be purchased by a family for about $20 to $30

Family-Friendly Resorts

St. Kitts Marriott Resort & The Royal Beach Casino

Location: St. Kitts Marriott Resort, Frigate Bay

Consider staying at the St. Kitts Marriott Resort if you want to travel with kids. It serves both adults and kids with its large pools, waterslide, and beachside setting.

The resort provides a Kids Club with activities overseen by staff, so parents may unwind while their small children explore on their own. There's family-friendly entertainment at the Royal Beach Casino as well.

Depending on the type of room and season, accommodations at the St. Kitts Marriott Resort normally cost between $200 and $400 per night. The resort provides many dining alternatives; meals and activities may incur additional fees.

Nevis's Four Seasons Resort

Location: Four Seasons Resort, Nevis

Travel to Nevis to discover the Four Seasons Resort's charming family atmosphere. This resort guarantees a wonderful stay for every family member with its roomy accommodations, Kids for All Seasons programme, and an assortment of family-friendly activities. The Four Seasons accommodates a range of interests for both parents and kids, including educational opportunities and water sports.

Depending on the season and the type of room, the Four Seasons Resort in Nevis offers luxurious lodging for $500 to $1,500 a night. The resort offers family-friendly activities; extra fees could apply for certain experiences and meals.

Activities for All Ages

Zip-lining at Sky Safari Adventures

Check out Sky Safari Adventures in St. Kitts for an exhilarating family experience. For both adults and children, zip-lining through the beautiful rainforest is an exciting experience. The licenced guides provide an educational element and guarantee safety, making it an engaging and unforgettable family activity.

The cost of a zip-lining adventure with Sky Safari Adventures is between $90 to $100 per person. The excitement of zip-lining through the rainforest is included, along with the bonus of knowledgeable guides who will ensure your safety and add an educational element to your journey.

Beach at Frigate Bay

Enjoy a peaceful day at the family-friendly Frigate Bay Beach, which has smooth sands and tranquil waves. Play in the water with the kids by making sandcastles or going paddleboarding. Beach bars and eateries line the shore, offering a handy and fun environment for a family outing.

For families, there is no cost involved in enjoying Frigate Bay Beach. Even if you may want to spend money on refreshments or water sports, everyone can enjoy a day of leisure on the soft sands for free.

Caribelle Batik at Romney Manor

Visit Caribelle Batik at Romney Manor in St. Kitts to learn about the craft of batik. Explore the verdant gardens with the whole family and take in the process of manufacturing batiks. Try your hand at batik to indulge your artistic side and bring home one-of-a-kind mementoes made by each member of the family.

It costs between $5 and $10 per person to experience Caribelle Batik at Romney Manor. This includes admission to the gardens, a look at how batik is produced, and the chance to make a batik work of art of your own.

There are several family-friendly activities available in St. Kitts and Nevis, ranging from exciting zip-lining excursions to picturesque train journeys.

Families of all sizes and ages may enjoy a warm and varied choice of activities on the islands, whether they are exploring bustling markets, relaxing on the beach, or taking in the native way of life.

Chapter 8

Travelling as Seniors

Senior-Friendly Accommodations and Transportation

The Ocean Terrace Inn

Location: Ocean Terrace Inn, Basseterre

The serene lodgings of Basseterre's Ocean Terrace Inn are well-known for their senior-friendly vibe. It meets the needs of seniors with comfortable rooms, accessible amenities, and a peaceful environment. The hotel staff can help plan excursion transportation, making your stay easy and stress-free.

Transportation Suitable for Seniors:

Use private transfers or trustworthy local taxi services for senior-friendly transportation. Comfortable solutions for elders are frequently offered by businesses such as Grey's Island Excursions. Private transportation might cost anywhere from $30 to $50, depending on the distance.

Health Considerations for Seniors

Healthcare Facilities

Learn where the hospitals and clinics are located. The primary healthcare facility on St. Kitts is the Joseph N. France General Hospital located in Basseterre. Nevis also boasts Alexandra Hospital. Basic consultations are affordable, but it's a good idea to get travel insurance that will pay for any unexpected medical costs.

Travellers' Insurance:

Seniors experiencing medical issues may think about purchasing travel insurance. Comprehensive travel insurance policies are available from companies such as

World Nomads and Allianz Travel; the cost of the plan varies from $50 to $150 based on the length of the trip and the coverage.

Relaxing Activities and Leisurely Tours

Romney Manor Gardens

Location: Romney Manor Gardens, St. Kitts

Discover the peaceful Romney Manor Gardens, a historic location surrounded by lovely gardens. Elderly people can take strolls through well-kept gardens and admire the beauty of exotic flora. With an estimated $5 admission fee, it's a cost-effective and culturally enriching event.

Brimstone Hill Fortress Shuttle

For a convenient means of accessing this UNESCO World Heritage Site, seniors can opt to use the shuttle service operated by Brimstone Hill Fortress. With a round-trip ticket of about $10, the shuttle guarantees a comfortable ride, giving elders a stress-free experience without requiring them to go a great distance.

Beautiful Drive to Nevis Peak

Consider taking a leisurely drive to see Nevis Peak as a picturesque activity. Seniors can appreciate Nevis's natural beauty from the comfort of a car with the help of several tour companies that offer island tours.

A guided island trip may cost between $50 and $100 per person, depending on the length of time and what's included.

Seniors can travel to St. Kitts and Nevis in comfort and at a reasonable price. Seniors can maximise their travel experience without sacrificing safety or fun by booking accommodations that cater to their needs, thinking ahead about health measures, and choosing leisure activities.

Always seek advice from medical specialists and knowledgeable travellers to guarantee a secure and fulfilling vacation.

Come on! There is no need to worry.

Chapter 9

Guide for First-Time Visitors

Arrival and Airport Tips

1. Robert L. Bradshaw International Airport (SKB) - St. Kitts

Fill out immigration and customs forms on the plane to expedite the admission process at Robert L. Bradshaw International Airport. Have a pen and the required paperwork on hand. Once you get through customs, you'll find various transportation options outside the airport, such as taxis and rental cars. To go to famous destinations like Basseterre, a taxi fare could cost you $20 to $30.

2. Vance W. Amory International Airport (NEV) - Nevis

Vance W. Amory International Airport is a friendly, modest airport for travellers arriving in Nevis. For easy transportation to your lodging, taxis are easily found outside and run between $15 and $25. The ferry is another picturesque alternative if travelling from St. Kitts; tickets run about $10 to $15.

Exchange of Currency

When you arrive, exchange some money for convenience. Although US dollars are commonly accepted, the official currency is the Eastern Caribbean Dollar (XCD). The use of major credit cards is very widespread. Exchange rates are subject to fluctuation, so it's best to check with nearby banks or exchange services to get the best deals.

Navigating Public Transportation

Taxi Services

For short trips and island tours, taxis are an easy way to get around. Before departing on your trip, confirm the fare and feel free to negotiate for a fair price. Taxis are typically available at airports and popular tourist destinations. For brief trips, expect to pay between $15 and $30 for a cab, with the price changing according to distance.

Car Rentals

Exploration is made more flexible when you rent a car. Make sure your driver's licence is up to date, and drive carefully on the left side of the road. Many rental companies provide a variety of car options, like Thrifty and Avis. Prices for renting a car range from $50 to $70 per day, depending on the kind of vehicle.

Public Buses

Although there are public buses, they may not be as handy or regular for visitors. For a more convenient and effective experience, taxis or rental cars are typically advised.

Common Tourist Mistakes to Avoid

Bringing Too Much With You

Don't overpack for your trip to the Caribbean. Because of the laid-back vibe of the islands, packing light, wearing swimwear, sunscreen, and a hat are necessities.

For outdoor activities, don't forget to bring insect repellent. You can prevent paying excessive baggage fees by packing wisely.

Ignoring The Local Customs

Honour regional traditions and customs. Wear modest clothing when you visit places of worship or nearby communities. Offer the locals a cordial "Good morning" or "Good afternoon," demonstrating consideration for their culture. It's a modest but impactful gesture.

Dismissing Sun Protection

The Caribbean sun has a strong ray. Always wear sunglasses, use sunscreen, and drink plenty of water. This is important, particularly if you are planning beach or outdoor activities. Depending on the type and SPF, sunscreen can range in price from $10 to $20.

Missing Local Food

Visit restaurants like Ballahoo Restaurant in Basseterre or Mr X's Shiggidy Shack in Nevis to sample the food of the area. Enjoy the opportunity to sample fresh seafood, regional fruits, and delectable Caribbean cuisine. At nearby eateries, a person's meal can cost anywhere from $15 to $40.

Neglecting Island Hopping

Consider island hopping if you have the time. For a day trip, take a ferry from St. Kitts to Nevis, or vice versa. Every island has a distinct charm and charms of its own. Ferry fares range from $10 to $15, so it's a scenic and reasonably priced experience.

Your first trip to St. Kitts and Nevis will go smoothly and leave you with wonderful memories if you follow this arrival advice, use transport carefully and steer clear of typical tourist blunders.

Without going above budget, take in the breathtaking scenery, the friendly hospitality of the islands, and the vibrant culture of the Caribbean.

Chapter 10

Sample Itineraries

3-Day Adventure Itinerary

Day 1: Discovery of the Island

Morning: Fly into Robert L. Bradshaw International Airport (SKB), then make your way to Basseterre to have a filling breakfast typical of the Caribbean.

To gain insight into the history of the island, pay a visit to Independence Square and the National Museum. To start your day, have a coffee at one of the neighbourhood cafes, such as Rituals Coffee House.

Afternoon: Proceed to Brimstone Hill Fortress National Park via a picturesque drive. Discover the beautifully restored fortress while taking in expansive views of St. Kitts and the surrounding islands. For a closer look at the island's varied flora and animals, consider hiking the neighbouring paths if you're feeling daring.

Evening: Go back to Basseterre and eat at a neighbourhood restaurant. Discover the vibrant vibe of Frigate Bay's The Strip, which is well-known for its bars and nightlife. To round off the evening perfectly, try one of Sunshine's Beach Bar's renowned 'killing bee' cocktails.

Day 2: Excursions Packed with Adrenaline

Morning: For an exhilarating experience, go zip-lining with Sky Safari Adventures. As you soar through the treetops, take in breathtaking panoramas of the rainforest. Use one of the GoPro rentals that are offered on location to record the action.

Afternoon: Spend a leisurely afternoon at the beach at South Friars Bay. Try some water sports like paddleboarding or snorkelling. Enjoy a beachside barbecue for lunch at Mr X's Shiggidy Shack, which is well-known for its vibrant ambience and mouth watering grilled delicacies.

Evening: Enjoy fresh seafood meals at a restaurant by the beach while taking in the sunset. For a unique night spent beneath the stars, think about attending a beach bonfire event.

Day 3: Day Trip to Nevis

Morning: From Basseterre, take a ferry to Nevis. Discover Nevis's capital, Charlestown, and pay a visit to the Museum of Nevis History. Don't pass up the chance to snap a selfie with the well-known statue of Alexander Hamilton.

Afternoon: Have lunch at a restaurant by the shore and unwind on Pinney's shore. For a taste of the real Caribbean, try the conch fritters or the renowned Nevisian lobster.

Evening: In the evening, head back to St. Kitts. Savour a goodbye meal at a waterfront restaurant in Basseterre while remembering your exciting days spent exploring the Caribbean.

5-Day Cultural Immersion Itinerary

Day 1: Arrival and Cultural Exposure

Afternoon: Arrive at Robert L. Bradshaw International Airport (SKB). After settling up, take a stroll through Basseterre to experience the local vibe. See the Berkeley Memorial, an emblem of the history of Kittitian.

Evening: Savour dinner at a neighbourhood eatery serving Caribbean food. Choose a meal such as "conch chowder" or "goat water" to begin your culinary adventure.

Day 2: Basseterre History

Morning: Take a tour of Berkeley Memorial, The Circus, and St. George's Anglican Church, three historic locations. Explore Basseterre's colonial past.

Afternoon: Investigate the Fairview Great House and Botanical Garden. Visit a neighbourhood market or a restaurant that serves real Caribbean food to have a genuine Kittitian meal.

Evening: Go to a play or other cultural event in the area. For a fully immersive experience, check the local event calendars for dance performances or music festivals.

Day 3: Kittitian Village Life and Brimstone Hill

Morning: Take a historical tour of Brimstone Hill Fortress National Park. Admire the fortress's engineering prowess and discover its historical significance in the Caribbean.

Afternoon: Visit a nearby Kittitian village, engage in conversation with the residents, and take part in cultural events. Take part in hands-on classes like cooking or traditional craft workshops.

Evening: For a real taste of the islands, have dinner in a restaurant with a Kittitian flair. For a tasty taste of the region's food, try the "stewed saltfish" or "spicy plantain chips".

Day 4: Cultural Day on Nevis

Morning: Go to Nevis by ferry. Investigate the Bath Hotel ruins and the Alexander Hamilton Museum. Explore the island's intriguing history.

Afternoon: Visit the Nevisian Heritage Village in the afternoon to learn more about Nevisian culture. Discover the island's native customs and take in traditional dance performances.

Evening: Take in a live music or dance event in the area. Attending a local music festival during your visit is highly recommended for an energetic evening filled with rhythms from the Caribbean.

Day 5: Exploring Arts and Crafts

Morning: Take in the beauty of Kittitian and Nevisian artwork by visiting nearby art galleries like the Dale Art Gallery or the Gallery Café. Talk to local artists and find out where they get their inspiration from.

Afternoon: Take part in a craft workshop to make your memento. Discover the craft of batik or basket making from knowledgeable craftspeople.

Evening: Have a farewell meal to round off your cultural experience. For a farewell dinner that will never be forgotten, pick a restaurant that combines fine dining with live local music.

Relaxing Beach Retreat: A 7-Day Itinerary

Day 1-2: Arriving there and unwinding on the beach

Afternoon: Arrive at Robert L. Bradshaw International Airport (SKB). After checking into your oceanfront hotel, relax. To get used to the calm atmosphere, take a stroll down the shore.

Evening: Have dinner at a neighbourhood eatery by the water. Enjoy grilled seafood while dining on the beach in the Caribbean beneath the stars.

Day 3-4: Beach Days at Frigate Bay

Whole Day: Visit Frigate Bay Beach during your stay. Take a nap, read a book, or go kayaking or snorkelling on the ocean. Get a beach cabana to enjoy breathtaking views of the ocean while being shaded.

Evenings: For a more relaxed vibe, check out The Strip's oceanfront eateries and bars. For a truly tropical evening, try some cocktails with a Caribbean influence and enjoy some live music.

Days 5 and 6: Rainforest Retreat and Scenic Railway

Morning: Enjoy the magnificent vistas while touring the St. Kitts Scenic Railway. Enjoy a tropical fruit cocktail or mimosa while you drive through these breathtaking scenes.

Afternoon: Spend a spa day and some downtime in a jungle hideaway. Get a massage while listening to the sounds of nature, or try a restorative yoga class.

Evening: Savour a peaceful supper at the retreat or a local eatery. For a tasty meal, try recipes with Caribbean influences that employ fresh vegetables from the area.

Day 7: Island Farewell

Morning: Savour the last moments of your retreat with a stroll down the beach in the morning. Gather seashells or construct a sandcastle to create a treasured memento.

Afternoon: With a heart full of Caribbean memories, head for the airport. Visit a nearby market to obtain last-minute keepsakes such as locally-made spices or handcrafted items.

On these enchanted Caribbean islands, adjustments can be made according to particular preferences, and every day promises new and amazing experiences.

Chapter 11

Useful Resources

Emergency Contacts

Emergency Services

- Police: 911
- Medical Emergency: 911
- Fire Department: 911

Medical facilities:

Joseph N. France General Hospital (St. Kitts)

- Address: Lime Kiln, Basseterre, St. Kitts
- Contact: +1 869-465-2551
- Emergency Room: For immediate medical needs, open around the clock.

Alexandra Hospital (Nevis)

- Address: Hospital Road, Charlestown, Nevis
- Contact: +1 869-469-5473
- Emergency Services: Ready to manage emergency medical situations.

Practical Apps for Vacationers

Transportation and Navigation

1. *Google Maps:* A dependable navigational aid that offers information on public transport and real-time traffic updates.
2. *Uber or Lyft:* Uber and Lyft are convenient and frequently affordable modes of transportation.
3. *XE Currency Converter:* You can remain up to date on the most recent currency conversion rates with the help of XE Currency Converter.

Communication

1. *Google Translate:* Transform spoken and written words into multiple languages to overcome communication hurdles.
2. *WhatsApp:* Don't worry, you can still use calls and messages to stay in touch with friends, family, and even locals.

Organising a Trip

1. *TripAdvisor:* Plan your journey with the help of other travellers' reviews, suggestions, and insights.
2. *SkyScanner:* Use Skyscanner to find and compare flight costs so you can get the best possible deal on your travels.

Safety and Health

1. *TravelSafe:* Be up to date on local safety advice, emergency numbers, and travel advisories.

2. *First Aid by American Red Cross:* The American Red Cross's First Aid provides helpful information on first aid techniques to help you be ready for any unexpected situations.

Suggested Reading and Additional Details

Books

A. "A Short History of St. Kitts and Nevis" by Sir Probyn Inniss:: This insightful book will help you comprehend the rich history of the islands on a deeper level.

B. "Island in the Sun" by Alec Waugh: Give yourself over to this timeless book that perfectly portrays life in the Caribbean.

Web-Based Resources

1. Visit the official tourism website (www.stkittstourism.kn) for insightful information, travel advice, and event schedules for St. Kitts and Nevis.
2. Nevis Tourism Authority (www.nevisisland.com): For information on Nevis, including travel information, sights, and events.

These resources work as your travelling companions, providing you with essential contacts, practical applications, suggested reading, and comprehensive information to guarantee a well-planned and pleasurable trip to St. Kitts and Nevis. When travelling, put safety first at all times and keep yourself informed.

Conclusion

Recap of Key Points

As you get ready to set out on your fantastic trip to the fascinating islands of St. Kitts and Nevis, let's review some essential details from this all-inclusive travel guide:

Introduction

A hidden Caribbean jewel, St. Kitts and Nevis attracts with its beautiful scenery, hospitable beaches, and rich cultural heritage.

Getting Started

A strong foundation is provided by essential travel knowledge, which makes sure you're ready for the journey ahead. Acquire a visa, learn about the subtleties of the local money, and enjoy the friendliness of the local tongue.

St Kitts and Nevis Travel Guide 2024

Planning Your Trip

Plan your trip by thinking about when it is ideal to visit the islands, bringing supplies for different activities, and putting your health and safety first. The islands provide a perfect balance of adventure and leisure.

Cultural Perspectives

Take in the colourful cultures of the Kittitian and Nevisian people. Accept regional traditions, observe manners, and partake in the exciting events that dot the island's calendar.

Top Must-See Destinations

Discover Basseterre, the capital city, a vibrant fusion of modern and historical architecture. Climb the Nevis Peak Hike for an exciting journey and ascend to Brimstone Hill Fortress National Park for expansive vistas.

Events and Activities

Enjoy the tastes of Kittitian and Nevisian cuisine, go on historical tours that reveal the stories of the islands, and dive into the crystal-clear seas for water sports. Insider knowledge elevates the experience of travelling alone and fosters a closer bond with the location.

Family-Friendly Adventures

Customise your family's vacation with plenty of family-friendly activities, kid-friendly attractions, and resorts. Together, make enduring memories while you explore.

Travelling as Senior

Enjoy peace of mind in senior-friendly lodgings, hassle-free transportation, and leisurely tours that are geared towards relaxation and soaking in the beauty of the islands.

Guide for First-Time Visitors

To guarantee a comfortable welcome to the islands, use public transit, navigate the arrival process with ease, and avoid common tourist mistakes.

Sample Itineraries

Take off on exhilarating 3-day excursions, immerse yourself in cultural learning with a 5-day schedule, or reward yourself with a weeklong beach getaway. Every itinerary guarantees a distinctive and rewarding experience.

Useful Resources

You can travel with peace of mind thanks to emergency contacts, suggested apps, and intelligent reading that expands your knowledge of the islands.

Wishing You a Spectacular Journey!

I hope your voyage to the sun-kissed coasts of St. Kitts and Nevis is full of exciting, breathtaking, and culturally immersive experiences. These islands have a lot to offer, from the lively districts of Basseterre to the tranquil beaches of Nevis.

Take part in exhilarating excursions, relish the distinctive tastes of the Caribbean, and allow the soul-stirring beats of regional music to enchant you. I'm wishing you an incredible journey full of memories that last long after the sun sets.

Good luck on your journey!

Made in United States
North Haven, CT
08 May 2024